This book
belongs to

_____

ON MY WAY WITH SESAME STREET™

Volume 6

Colors and Shapes

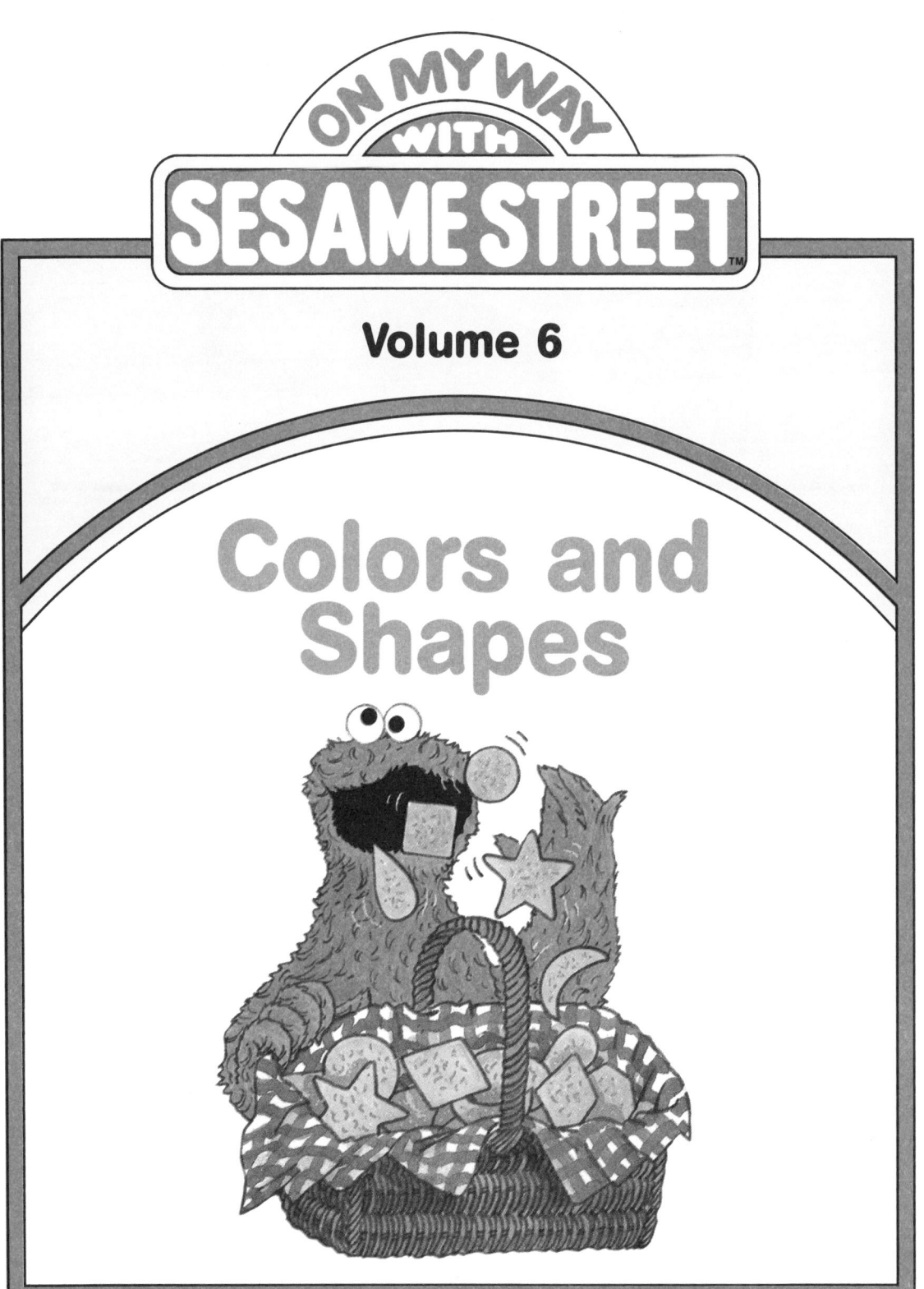

Featuring Jim Henson's Sesame Street Muppets

Children's Television Workshop/Funk & Wagnalls

Authors

Linda Hayward
Valjean McLenighan
Michaela Muntean
Emily Thompson
Pat Tornborg

Illustrators

Tom Brannon
Richard Brown
Tom Cooke
Robert Dennis
Tom Leigh
Joe Mathieu
Kimberly A. McSparran
Maggie Swanson

A Parents' Guide to COLORS AND SHAPES

Distinguishing COLORS AND SHAPES helps children to sort and classify objects. They can match the red socks or stack the square blocks, for example. These are basic preschool skills.

Recognizing and naming colors also helps children communicate about the world around them. They can say, "I want to wear my yellow sweater," for example.

Learning about shapes helps children begin to perceive the configurations that make up letters and numbers — important pre-reading and pre-math skills.

"Who Ever Heard of a Purple Puppy?" is a story that presents colors in their natural context: blueberries that are blue and oranges that are orange. It also shows that sometimes the sky can be pink and a tree can be yellow — just like in Ernie's drawing.

In "Big Bird's Square Meal," the whole gang goes on a picnic. They eat square sandwiches, round pies, and oval pieces of watermelon on a square tablecloth — or at least they try to!

Activities such as "Circle Circus" and "Square Fair" encourage children to find shapes in the pictures.

We hope your children will enjoy discovering the colors and shapes in the world around them.

**The Editors
SESAME STREET BOOKS**

Who Ever Heard of a Purple Puppy?

Saturday morning, when Ernie and Bert woke up, it was raining.
"What shall we do today?" asked Bert.
"I know," said Ernie, "let's color!" Bert got down his crayons and
Ernie pulled out some paper. They both worked hard on their pictures.

"All done," said Bert.

"What did you draw, Bert?" asked Ernie. Bert proudly held up his picture of a gray pigeon sitting in a green tree against a bright blue sky.

"Let's see yours," said Bert. Ernie held up his picture.

"It's a nice picture, Ernie," said Bert, "but you made the sky pink! Sky isn't pink, it's blue. Trees aren't yellow. They're green like the tree in my picture. And who ever heard of a purple puppy?"

"Just use your imagination, Bert," said Ernie.

"Oh, sure, Ernie," said Bert. "I can see that I need to teach you about colors."

Just then the sun peeked out, and the sky turned a brilliant blue. Ernie and Bert raced outside. "See, Ernie, the sky is blue," said Bert. "And here is Grover. He is blue, too."

"Oh, I am not blue," said Grover. "I am happy because my grandmonster sent me this cute and adorable blue jean jacket."

"No, no, Grover," said Bert. "I didn't mean that you felt blue. I meant that the color of your fur is blue."

"That is true," said Grover. "Would you like a blueberry?"

"Cowabunga!" said another blue monster. "Someone say blueberry?"

RRRrrreee-OOOooowww! screamed the siren of a red fire engine as it roared past. Everyone turned to watch, including Elmo, who was carrying a bag of groceries home from the store. He walked right into a fire hydrant and dropped the groceries—SPLAT—onto the sidewalk. Ernie and Bert ran to help.

"Oh, look," said Bert. "These apples and tomatoes are another important color. They're red, just like that fire engine."

"Elmo's red, too," said Ernie.

"Right, old buddy," said Bert. "You're catching on."

"Taxi! Oh, taxi, yoo-hoooo!" yelled Big Bird
from the corner.

"Where are you going, Big Bird?" asked Ernie.

"I'm taking these flowers to Granny Bird
for her birthday," said Big Bird.

"Never mind that, Ernie," said Bert. "Look, this is great! Notice
Big Bird—a yellow bird—holding yellow daffodils, getting into a
yellow cab. Now, that makes a
beautiful picture."

"Thank you," said Big Bird.
"Good-bye!"

"Now, let's see," said Bert.
"I've taught you about blue,
red, and yellow. What can I
show you that's orange?
Ernie, your ORANGE is the
color orange!"

"Gee, Bert," said Ernie.
"Orange you glad I bought
an orange? Hee, hee, hee!"

As Ernie and Bert walked by Oscar's trash can, they heard a terrible crashing and clanging of lids.

"Oh, yeah?" grouched Oscar.

"Yeah!" yelled Grungetta.

"Says who?" asked Oscar.

"Says me!" screamed Grungetta.

"Uh, excuse me," said Bert.

"WHAT DO YOU WANT?" yelled Oscar and Grungetta.

"I just wanted to show Ernie something green, and you two are perfect examples. See, Ernie—Oscar and Grungetta are green like leaves on a tree, or grass, or vegetables like broccoli, green beans, peas..."

"Hey," said Oscar. "Who are you calling perfect?"

"Yeah," said Grungetta. "Who?"

"We'll just be going now," said Ernie.

CRASH! The two trash can lids slammed shut.

Then Ernie and Bert heard a crash coming from the arbor area. They walked over to investigate.

"Don't worry," said Prairie Dawn. "I just knocked over our sign."

"Here, let me help you," said Bert as he picked up the sign from the sidewalk. "Frosty Fruit Fizzies. Ten cents," he read.

"That's right," said Prairie. "Telly and I are going into business. What flavor would you like: grape, lime, orange, lemon, cherry, or blueberry?"

"I'll take one grape, please," said Bert. Prairie Dawn poured him a tall cup of juice, and Bert handed over a dime. "Now, here's another neat color, Ernie. Grape juice is purple like grapes, or eggplants, or violets."

Just then Barkley and some of his puppy friends dashed around the corner, chasing a ball.

"See?" Bert told Ernie. "Puppies can be white, or black, or brown, or sometimes all three. But they are never purple."

The ball rolled right between Bert's feet. The little white puppy dived after it, knocking the cup from Bert's hand. Grape juice splashed all over the puppy.

"Look, Bert," said Ernie, laughing. "A purple puppy!"

"Now I've seen everything!" said Bert.

Let's Yell Yellow!

Let's yell yellow!
Let's say hello.
Let's find four yellow things
In the picture below.

Find the four yellow things in the picture.

Which yellow thing would you peel and slice and put on your cereal?

Which yellow thing would you put on toast?

Which yellow thing would you use to make lemonade?

Which yellow thing would you put on a hot dog?

Mustard

The Count's Fireworks

White Rabbits

White is for rabbits,
For clouds and for snow.
Can you find the rabbits
In the picture below?

The Amazing Mumford has lost his rabbits.
Help Grover find them.

How many rabbits did you find?

Bert's Collections

LOOK, ERNIE! I HAVE THREE COLLECTIONS-- A COLLECTION OF BROWN THINGS, A COLLECTION OF GRAY THINGS, AND A COLLECTION OF PINK THINGS. ISN'T THAT GREAT?

GEE, BERT, I BET THAT NO ONE ELSE IN THE WHOLE WORLD HAS A COLLECTION OF BROWN THINGS **AND** A COLLECTION OF GRAY THINGS **AND** A COLLECTION OF PINK THINGS. YOU'LL BE FAMOUS.

What belongs in Bert's collection of BROWN THINGS?
What belongs in Bert's collection of GRAY THINGS?
What belongs in Bert's collection of PINK THINGS?
Which box is the box for them?

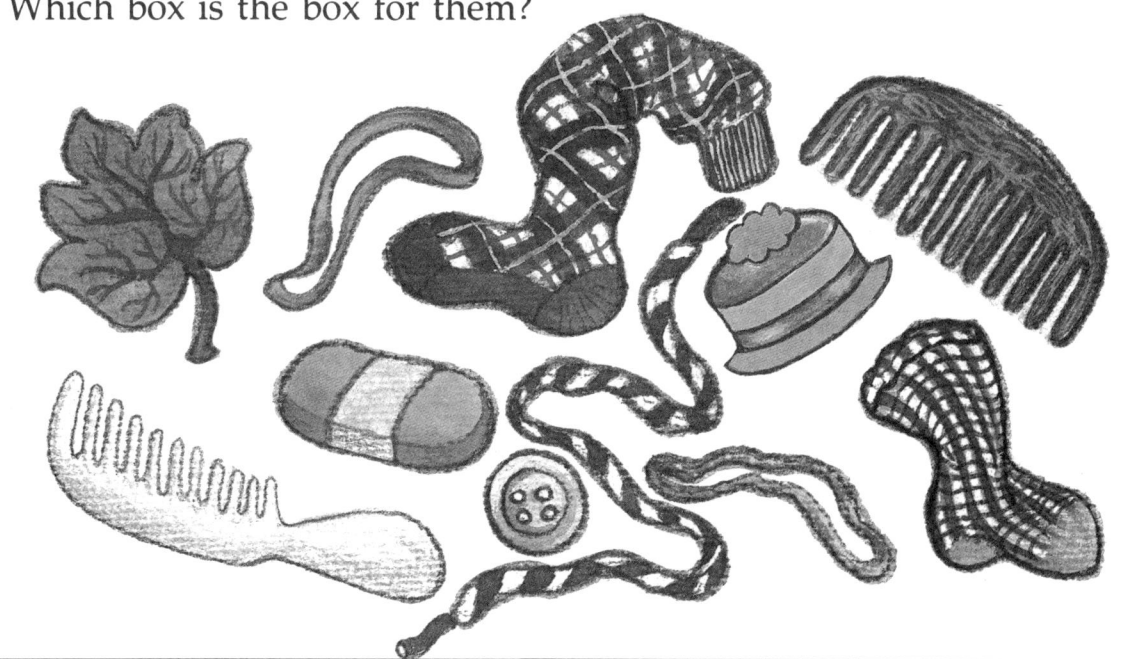

Ernie's Work of Art

Color Match

Point to something yellow to eat.

Point to something green to wear on your feet.

Point to something to play with that is red.

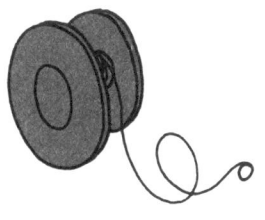   

Point to something blue to wear on your head.

   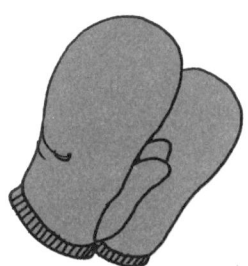

Follow the Colors

Purple plums
And purple grapes,
Seven purple polka dots
On a pair of purple drapes.

Follow the purple grapes to find something purple to drink.

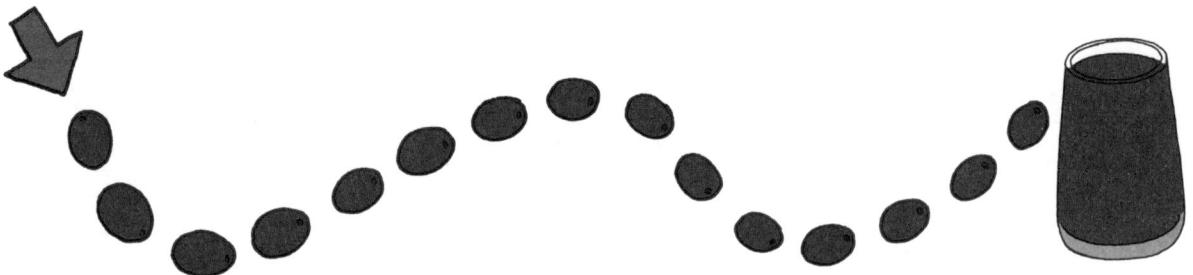

Follow the oranges to find something orange to drink.

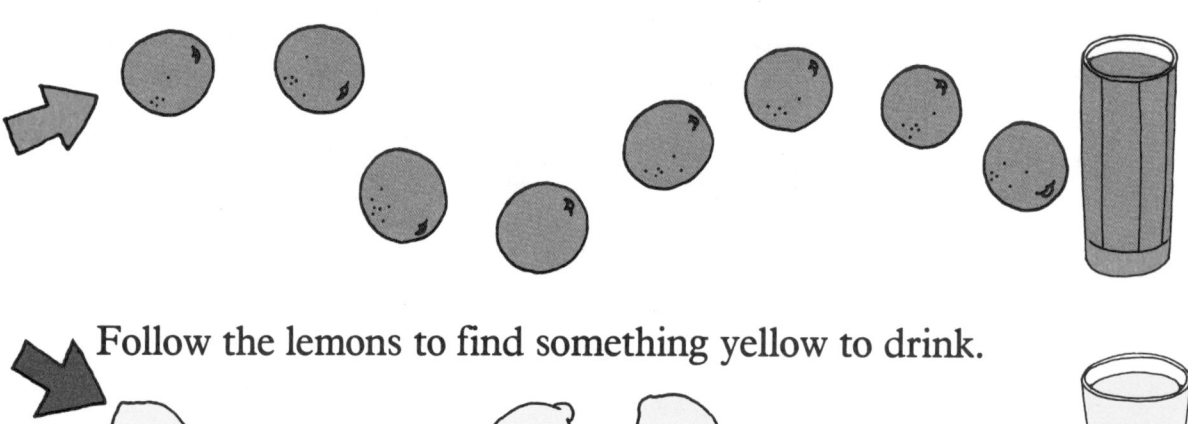

Follow the lemons to find something yellow to drink.

Bean Green

To serve two—

Note: Adult supervision is suggested.

What you need:

1 10-ounce can of green beans, or 1 cup of
fresh or frozen beans, cooked and cooled

⅓ cup of sweet pickle relish

1 green onion stem, cut with scissors

2 teaspoons of lemon juice

What you do:

Mix all the ingredients together. Then let the
Bean Greens cool in the refrigerator for an
hour before you eat them.

At the Laundromat

We take our clothes and wash them at
The Wishy-Washy Laundromat.

We put clothes in the washing machine,
And add some soap; they come out clean.

Then round and round the dryer goes,
Blowing warm air on wet clothes.
When it stops, you'll know why —
All the clothes are nice and dry.

Betty Lou is
helping her daddy
fold the clothes.

Which color socks
go together?

Uh, oh! One sock
is missing. Can
you find it in the
picture?

Art Class

"Painting, drawing,
Modeling clay —

Look what I made
In art class today!"

This is the picture that Grover painted.

Match the red paint to the red thing in the picture.

Match the blue paint to the blue thing in the picture.

Match the yellow paint to the yellow thing in the picture.

Match the green paint to the green thing,
the orange paint to the orange thing, and
the purple paint to the purple thing in the picture.

Colors and Shapes

The Sesame Street Players are getting ready to put on a show. Can you guess what the play will be?

The Sesame Street Players PRESENT "HANSEL and GRETEL" STARRING ERNIE and BERT

Can you find these colors in the picture?

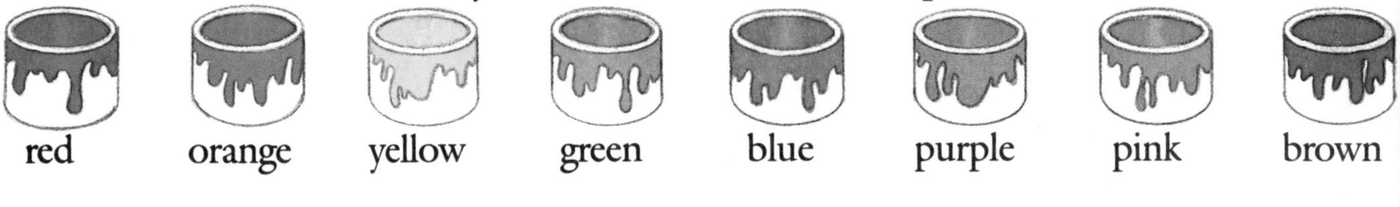

 red

 orange

yellow

 green

 blue

 purple

 pink

 brown

Can you find these shapes in the picture?

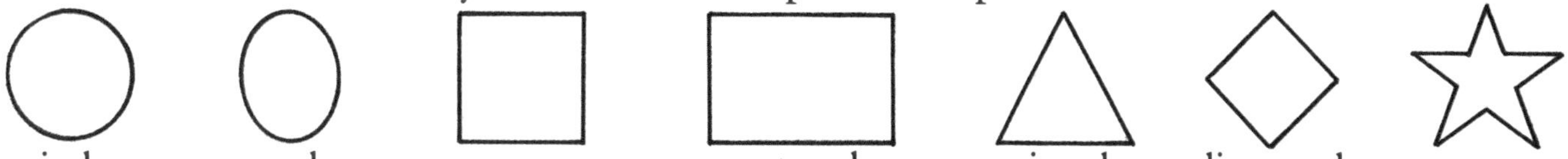

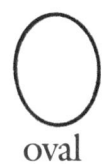 circle 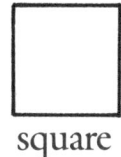 oval  square 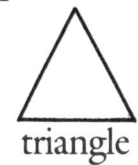 rectangle  triangle  diamond star

Big Bird's Square Meal

"Oh, my little Big Bird!" said Granny Bird as she arrived at Big Bird's nest. "How you've grown!"

"Thanks, Granny," said Big Bird. "I can't wait for our picnic."

"Come, then, dear," said Granny. "Cookie Monster and Elmo are waiting."

"What's in your basket, Granny?" asked Big Bird as they settled on a green grassy spot next to the pond.

"I've packed a good square meal for us!" said Granny.

"I know all about squares—and other shapes, too!" said Elmo.

"Okay, Elmo," said Big Bird. "What shape is this tablecloth?"

"A rectangle!" said Elmo.

"Right, Elmo," said Granny. "But look what happens when I unfold it."

"Now it's a square," said Elmo, "with little red-and-white squares all over it."

"Here are some peanut-butter-and-jelly sandwiches," said Granny.

"Look! More squares!" said Elmo.

"PICNIC!" cried Cookie Monster.

He bit into a sandwich.

"Now all that's left of the square sandwich is a triangle," said Big Bird.

"Who knows what shape this is?" asked Granny.

"It looks like a squashed circle," said Big Bird.

"It's not a circle," said Elmo. "This pie is a circle. See? It's round."

"This watermelon piece is an oval," said Elmo.

"Give me oval!" said Cookie as he gobbled up the watermelon.

"Now, here's an important shape," said Elmo, holding up his milk carton. "It's called a pentagon."

"Cowabunga! Give me pentagon!" said Cookie as he gobbled down the milk, carton and all.

"Now it's not a pentagon," said Big Bird. "It's just gone like the rest of our picnic."

"What's in your bag, Cookie Monster?"

rectangle

square

circle

oval

triangle

pentagon

"More shapes!" said Elmo. "Not shapes," said Cookie Monster, "COOKIES!"

"COWABUNGA!" his friends cried. "He's right!" And they gobbled up the rectangles and squares and triangles and circles and ovals and pentagons.

Triangle Park

Can you find nine triangles in this picture?

Circle Circus

Can you find nine circles in this picture?

Square Fair

Can you find ten squares in this picture?

Cookie Monster's Cookie Shapes

Rectangle Room

Can you find eight rectangles in this picture?

Grover's Shape Poem

Now that I know about shapes,
I see them wherever I look.
I see that the stamp is a square;
There's a rectangle-shape to my book!
The clock's face is a circle.
The pizza's a circle, too,
But I'll cut you a slice,
And then you tell me
What shape
It looks like to you!